I0202382

Exhale Midlife
Body Blues

6 Steps to Loving Your Body
at Midlife and Beyond

KATHERINE "KAT" FORSYTHE, MSW

Exhale Midlife Body Blues:
6 Steps to Loving Your Body at Midlife and Beyond
By Katherine "Kat" Forsythe, MSW

ISBN 978-0-9839750-3-8

©2013 Katherine Forsythe, MSW

World rights reserved. No part of this publication may be reproduced, stored in a retrieval system or transmitted, in any form or by any means, electronic, mechanical, photocopying, recording or otherwise for public use, including Internet applications, without the prior permission of the author except by a reviewer who may quote brief passages in a review to be printed in a magazine, newspaper or on the Web.

Published by Second Wind Publishing
www.getasecondwind.com
info@getasecondwind.com

Table of Contents:

Exhale Mid-Life Body Blues 6 Steps to Loving Your Body at Mid-Life and Beyond

A Journey Guide for Women

Before we begin:

What's the Point of This Personal Journey Guide, anyway?

"Change is inevitable. Growth is optional."

– UNKNOWN

The whole raison d'être for creating this personal journey guide is this: I wanted tools to rearrange our thinking from woe to wonderful - when we start to go south on self-confidence about our midlife and beyond bodies. Times like:

- In that cute little boutique fitting room - whether we're trying on:
  - lingerie (the worst)
  - bathing suits (a close second to lingerie — rated worse by some women)
  - business suit (even pricey high fashion doesn't protect us from body blues).

Then, there are these other awkward moments:

- When we undress for the first time in front of a new lover
- When we stand next to a lovely and firm 35 year old
- When we see our reflections in the wrong light at the hair salon
- When we see ourselves mirrored in the airport restroom.

Do these sound familiar? You're not alone.

I've shared the angst. Seven years ago at age 57, I stood in front of a mirror and faced myself full on. Staring back at me was someone I didn't like. She was tired. Her brow was furrowed. There were regret, displeasure and resentment in her eyes.

Look at that belly! And those drooping eyes! I began to cry. I was aging, and I didn't know what to do about it.

All the euphemisms for getting old bubbled up and left me with a big knot in my stomach: "mature?" "seasoned?" "aging gracefully?" "woman of wisdom?" "crone (oh, please, really?)". I didn't want to be any of those. I wasn't any of those!

I was a vibrant, zesty, sexy lady. Or so I thought. But this mirror episode was portraying the opposite. All the insecurities from my recent divorce came cascading down around me. I was over the hill. I had lost the edge. I was alone. I was getting old.

Then, something very poignant happened. As I was having this profound pity party, I looked up on my office bookshelf and saw a truism that my daughter had framed for me after the divorce. It simply said, "I came to live out loud."

At that moment, I made a resolve. Like Scarlet O'Hara vowing never to be hungry again, I promised myself to find a way out of this miserable despair and hopelessness that I felt over age gain – and to be a confident, sophisticated, beautiful and sexy woman, again, for the rest of my life.

Yes, my divorce had eaten away at my sense of self, but I was still the captain of this ship. I had a lifetime of skills to tackle this formidable foe.

I set about crafting a step by step recipe for myself to escape out of this quagmire of insecurity. I used all my professional resources from years of sales training and communication skills coaching, my years of relationship-fixing as a therapist, my knowledge of human behavior and sexuality from my MSW – and combined it all with

"To love oneself is the beginning of a lifelong romance."
-OSCAR WILDE

> *"You can wait and hope for a miracle. But miracles are so unpredictable."*
>
> —PETER DRUCKER

my personal wisdom gained from a tsunami of experiences in my life so far.

I created my own A 6 step guide to feeling wonderfull about who I was right now — smack dab in the middle of life, changing body and all!

It worked. I was feeling better. My friends asked me if I had some "work" done (plastic surgery). I answered that I had not, but had developed my own recipe for "anti-aging". They wanted in. I told them it wasn't about needles or knives, salves or supplements, food or fitness. It was about what was going on between my ears. I shared my 6 steps with them. It worked for them, too.

Now, I'm passionate about sharing what I developed with all of us who are challenged by the midlife struggle with our bodies and our feelings about ourselves. I want to share it with you, too. It's not magic. It's not a panacea. It will take some work, focus, and commitment. It requires honesty, and a real desire to get past our obsession with losing the youthfulness of our bodies — and the melancholy that comes with that, so that we are free to start feeling sexy and delicious all over again.

You can do this!

Let's be real. I'd like to go into that fitting room just once and actually relish it. I want to look 25 again, don't you? Okay, I'll go for 35. Never mind, forget it. Let's do 45. Truly, I don't want to see myself with cottage-cheese thighs, the muffin top waist, the chicken neck, the droopy eyes, the jowls. Shall I go on? You know the drill. I want to look younger and so do you. End of discussion. Wouldn't it be remarkable to have a system in place that allowed us to be comfortable in our skin — no matter what?

That's what this recipe for reclaiming our bodies, is about. It's going to position us to move forward in our uncharted lives after menopause - confidently, buoyantly, and vibrantly (not to mention

– with a little juiciness, too!). All the while, showing off a new 'tude, and walking into our lives with strength and verve.

Some women seem to naturally exude comfort and confidence after menopause, at 50 or 60 or 70 or 80. It's refreshing and encouraging to see healthy, robust 50, 60, 70, 80+ women. I get excited when an ebullient, confident, magnificent woman in the second half of life strolls by. She's a living example of my life's work passion – getting us to feel comfortable in our own skin, no matter what. We need more women like her - to be seen, to speak up, to be honest about the frustration of being viewed as invisible in our youth centric culture, and to exemplify the self-assurance that we all are seeking.

But honestly, out of the hundreds of women I've worked with, including that poised lady above, very few of us are happy with the way we look naturally—no matter what age we are. Most of us want to be told we look at least ten years younger. Very few of us want to be described this way: "She looks healthy, robust, and beautiful (so far, so good) *and* she really looks her age (ouch)!" Do you know that in my women's groups, 25% of women could not identify one single attribute they liked about their bodies? This is not good.

You and I have had countless conversations, and great belly laughs, over our escapades to recapture our youthful loveliness in these new bodies. We've felt some deep grief over the loss of youth, too. Letting go of the way we were, and accepting the way we are, is not a simple task. There are a whole host of physical indicators that tell us we are getting older - butts sag, breasts drop, bellies form, faces fall, eyes droop, skin dries out, and lubrication fades. And we don't like it. Aging gracefully? Not in this culture, if we can help it, and if Madison Avenue has its way.

"I couldn't wait for success so I decided to go ahead without it."
– JONATHON WINTERS

> *"Those who would have nothing to do with thorns must never attempt to gather flowers"*
> – Unknown

We have no role models.

We really don't know what "aging gracefully" means. We're once again the generation carving the first path to healthy and delicious living in the 2nd half of life. This time we're determined to make body aging a hurdle we can overcome. We want healthy age-gain. Really, we want to stay as young looking as we possibly can. We want to stop aging, or do the impossible: anti-aging. Off we go, determined to make it happen - solving it, analyzing it, taming it.

We're encountering a big obstacle, however. Since no generation has lived as long as we have – as healthy, confident, independent, strong women, we have no role models. We really don't know what to do with this new found predicament of health, independence, strength, confidence, and uncertain body image, all at once. We don't know who we're supposed to be.

The landscape today:
3 Profiles for "How to age gracefully"

In my work with women, I've found these interpretations of how to evolve as a woman at midlife and beyond:

- The Zen Woman. She says: *"Isn't it interesting? It will all work out the way the Universe intends it to be. Let the natural process take its course. I breathe, I do yoga, I take herbs."*

- The Not Me Woman: *"I'm not giving in. Are you kidding? I'm working out like a mad woman and I'm showing off this tight body through great clothes."*
Or...
"Better living through chemistry and modern medicine! Give me the knife and let the plastic surgeon work her magic."

- The Grandma Woman: *"It doesn't matter anymore because I don't need to be sexy. I need to be age appropriate. I have my grandkids to think about. I have garden club and I need to drive soccer car pool for my daughter.*"

Then there are the rest of us. *Truth told, we're a combination of all of these.* We don't fit neatly into any one category. We vacillate between all of these.

At the end of the day, we have 4 concerns that seem to be true for just about all of us:

- We don't want to be invisible. We want to continue to turn heads and to be seen as appealing, desirable, energized, attractive women.
- We don't want to be deemed obsolete.
- We don't want to lose the power from our younger years.
- We don't want the changes that are happening to our bodies.

What can we do about it? The good news is that there *is* something we *can* do about it! That's what this guide is for.

Here's how to use this guide. I suggest you start with Step 1 and motor all the way through step 6. It's a worthwhile drive. However, if you are less inclined travel the entire distance, feel free to flip through the pages to find what you need. Personalize this for yourself. In the end, it's your journey. When something resonates, read it, and do it.

The 6 Steps

- Step #1 is *Accept.* What's your attitude today? First you have to look at what you believe about yourself, and what you love/dislike about your body right now. There are some poignant surprises for you, believe me.

> *"So many women just don't know how great they really are. They come to us all vogue outside and vague inside."*
> – MARY KAY ASH

- *Adjust* is Step 2. Boost that point of view of yours to a fun, buoyant, vibrant, different level. You're going to love this step!

- Step 3 is *Appreciate.* A little applause for that hard working body of yours! This body has toiled hard for you for all these years. Perhaps a meaningful way of saying thank you is called for. Here's how you say, "Thank you, body of mine. I sure have put you through it, and I appreciate your tolerance!"

- *Adorn,* Step 4, means treating ourselves to new drapery for our newly appreciated, exquisite bodies. We have much to thank our amazing bodies for. Ornamenting ourselves with lovely accoutrements - and intensifying our upbeat thoughts is only the beginning.

- Step 5 is *Admire.* Here's where we talk about all the tricks and tips you can do to reclaim, redefine, and re-energize yourself.

- Step 6 is *Always: How To Do This For The Rest Of Your Life* (seriously.) Here's the secret to anti-aging. The secret is very, very easy to do, but here's the catch: You have to do it! If you want to stay youthful for the rest of your life, you have to keep doing Step 6. No equipment needed, except your brain and your commitment!

It's an easy guide to follow. It's a map that will get you from misery over sags and cellulite to feeling splendorific about yourself. It works. Period.

What it takes to make this work for you

No doubt, you've experienced countless weight management and/or exercise plans in your lifetime. In the process, you learned the following: No system works unless the following 5 conditions exist:

1. You want the system to work.
2. You are willing to put out the effort to make it work.
3. You have support in place to help you.
4. You can do it for the rest of your life.
5. You are willing to *actually do it*, day after day.

You can do this! I will show you how.

This handbook finishes with an invitation for you to join our deliciously fun — and life changing - community where you will find support, sharing, laughter, and learning. That's everything you need to move forward in your new mindset. We have an absolute blast!

There is vibrant, delicious online community, a "live" community, and newsletters, inspirational messages, webinars, books, CDs and everything else you can think of — all to support you.

We talk about the challenges with post-menopause bodies. We share the tsunami of change we've all been through in our lives. We capture the mindset and techniques to handle it all. You'll come away invigorated, entertained, feeling confident, and chortling to yourself.

"The experience of being on unfamiliar ground, of doing things differently is frightening. It always was and always will be. People handle their fear of change in different ways, but the fear is inescapable if they are, in fact, to change."

—M Scott Peck, MD.
From The Road
Less Traveled.

"If you're not scared, you're not doing it right."

— COMMENT ABOUT STARTING OVER LATE IN LIFE.

Enjoy this personal journey guide and make it work for you.

You deserve it! As I say at my events, it's time to take back ownership of our bodies. Take a deep breath and Own It! Exhale your Mid-Life body blues.

You're not getting older, you're getting started!™

Kat Forsythe

January 5, 2013

Your Notes

Step 1.

Accept

*"If it's to be,
it's up to me"*

-A FAVORITE OLD SAYING

Accepting the naked truth (and moving delightfully on)

The Belly Drama Begins

I don't know about you, but I've been disliking parts of my body all my life. I remember as a teenager sunbathing at my Aunt Kay's pool near Detroit. Mind you, I was a competitive swimmer who worked out strenuously every day. I was not fat.

But there I was, in my green two-piece bathing suit lying on a lawn chaise (the aluminum kind woven with the plastic ribbons in a plaid effect) when my five-year-old niece, Missy, came up to me and asked, "Kathy, is there a baby in your tummy?" At age 16, in that split second, I learned the meaning of "out of the mouths of babes." Horrified, I looked down to see what was showing up as a huge abnormal mound of flesh in my lower abdomen.

After I told her I was not pregnant, I waited for the death blow—asking me what that bulge was from, if not a baby. Blessedly, she lost interest in my fat stomach and skipped away. But her unabashed honesty confirmed what I had feared most: the whole world noticed my protruding belly.

How could I ever get a boyfriend sporting belly fat like that?

Today, as an adult, I can reframe her comment from a grown-up perspective. Nonetheless, I still carry the wound of overreaction to the flat out truth that I feared the most at 16: someone confirmed out loud that I had a big fat stomach.

The Truth

The truth is that there is nothing abnormal about the size of my tummy, actually. Nonetheless, if you have carried unnecessary sensitivity through the years, adopting a realistic adult view can be difficult. For me, I look around on a regular basis to see who else has a big tummy. I want company. That's not the adult attitude I need. We can learn to rethink our insecurities.

It's highly possible you've carried body issues with you, too, since childhood—or perhaps some have appeared with age. Naturally, yours are different than mine, but they might still cause you to obsess. For example, for me, I'm small-breasted and big-tummied (my obsession). As I swing up and down the weight scale, those two body parts seem to grow disproportionately—that is, the breasts tend to get smaller while the tummy gets bigger. I spend many moments in front of my mirror, standing at the right angle, of course, to see if anything has improved since the last time I checked (usually the night before).

What disappointment; nothing has changed.

By this time in our lives, we're the net sum of our experiences in life when it comes to how we think of ourselves. I was told by my brother that I wasn't just hit by the ugly stick. In fact, the whole ugly tree fell on me. He was 13 and I was 10.

Now it's your turn. I'm going to jog your memory and get you to tell yourself what inspiring messages you got from your past, and which ones have caused you a lifetime of misery. We all have those – even the most confident and beautiful of us. Together, we can save the good messages, and kick the others out of our lives forever.

Let's do it!

"When I say Own It!, I'm talking about taking personal ownership of how you consciously decide to articulate your own womanhood – how you step out – how you show up in the world. Own that!"

– KAT FORSYTHE

MIGHTY STRONG MESSAGES FROM THE PAST

- How were you supposed to live in your body, as a woman?
- What were you told about yourself that made you feel beautiful?
- What has stung you?
- Who said what to you?

We all got bright and dark messages. Is it time to stop listening to old tapes? Let's look:

What significant messages about my body did I get from:	What is the message?	Helpful! Remember this! (√)	Hurtful! (It was about them, not you!) (√)	I need a plan to stop listening (√)
Family messages (Bright and/or dark messages or events)				
Family DNA: What genes have you inherited?				
Personal life events not family related(bright and/or dark events in childhood, teen, early adult years, midlife)				
Ethnic/Cultural messages				
Spirituality/Religion				
My Own Personality				
Friendships – messages from girlfriends				
Partners: What did your love interests say?				
Education - teachers				
Worldwide historical events				

Voices came from all directions. What still helps? What messages need to go directly into the Goodwill Bag with a hearty "sayonara!"?

THE TSUNAMI OF CHANGE

You're a treasure chest of life experience. You bring a whole palette of colorful experiences to your life today. Some good, some not so great! All of them – the good, the great, the bad, the ugly – are the depth of you, the roots of you, the foundation of you. Give yourself a little credit for all that you have experienced, and the wisdom, fears, joys, and lenses for looking at life that you've gathered along the way.

"A ship is safe in the harbor, but that's not what it's meant for."
-WINSTON CHURCHILL

What's important is this:

The net sum of your life experience has molded, shaped, humbled, manipulated, built, and contributed to who you are today – RIGHT NOW - and how you feel about yourself and your body TODAY. Don't underestimate the power of all the events you have lived through.

Exhaling body blues means first glancing back briefly to see where you've come from – before you move forward. It's understanding the shades and hues of who you have become so you know what to bring with you moving forward, and what to leave in the dust.

The Tsunami Check List

You've been through massive changes, adjustments, and life altering experiences since your early 20's. It's time to look at them.

This is not about doom and gloom. This is about getting a handle on your life lessons that have influenced your attitudes, your opinions, and the way you step out in the world today. The joy comes in keeping what's worth keeping, blowing the rest away, and moving on.

The Tsunami Check List: Check all that apply.

NOTE: All of these life events are not equal in value, nor do they appear in order of importance. Some will apply to you, some not.

	Long term Marriage(s) or partnerships
	Marriage or partnership after a lifetime of flying solo (single)
	Living years with abusive partner
	Living years with partner with any of these challenges Long term illness: Disease: Mental challenges: Addiction:
	Supporting family for years
	Flying Solo (being single) and navigating life by yourself
	Raising children alone
	Raising children with any of the following challenges for years Long term illness: Disease: Mental challenges: Social challenges:
	Your own personal health profile Long term illness: Disease: Chronic physical conditions: Mental health challenges (depression, etc)

	Death of spouse
	Loss of child
	Death of parent(s)
	Death of significant person in your life
	Suicide of significant person in your life
	Extramarital affairs (yours or partner's)
	Divorce
	Significant friendship breakups
	The Unthinkable: anything that would cause most people to recoil, yet you experienced unwittingly, such as rape, murder, torture, watching an event you could not stop, etc.
	Relocating to a new place to live
	Starting your life all over again after death, divorce, illness, etc.
	Children leaving home
	Children coming back home to live as adults
	Financial disasters that blew your life apart
	Financial windfalls that changed your standard of living.
	Major decisions that turned out to be ghastly mistake and changed the course of your life:
	Other major events

Look at that! Pretty remarkable, all you have been through, isn't it? Don't you dare discount any of it, or compare yourself to anyone else. Yours has been a most distinctly unique journey!

CLAP, CLAP, CLAP for you, and all that you have weathered! Good job! You are an amazing woman, you know that?

How do you feel today?

Let's fast forward to right now. All those events that shaped you, all those messages you were given… all of them create the "you" today.

What's your attitude about yourself and your body today? Take this T/F quiz to get some perspective.

T or F	Question
	I have a favorite body part and I can easily name it.
	When I look in the mirror, I see an attractive **unclothed** body.
	When I look in the mirror, I see an attractive **clothed** body.
	I know exactly which styles of clothes compliment my body, and I'm assertive about seeking these styles.
	I never make apologies for my body (weight gain, weight loss, illness, injury, etc).
	I always simply say "thank you" when someone compliments me.
	I compliment other women every day.
	I don't compare myself to other women.
	I feel comfortable wearing a bathing suit when on vacation.
	I would never end a relationship because of the way my body looks.
	If I had plastic surgery, it would be because I wanted it, not for anyone else.
	I stand up straight, shoulders back, breasts out.
	I love my life.
	I see the future optimistically.

Score: There are no right or wrong answers, only those which you need to pay attention to. Which of these questions made you say "hmmmmm?" - bothered you, alerted you, or made you reconsider? Circle those!

THE NAKED TRUTH.

What we like. What we don't like. Time to zero in on Body Parts.

- Which body parts make you happy?
- Where do Your Worst Nightmares lurk?

Body part	I like it	I don't like it	Body part	I like it	I don't like it
Body in general			Back		
Face in general			Buttocks		
Hair			Arms		
Cheeks			Elbows		
Eyes			Hands		
Nose			Fingers		
Lips			Thighs		
Ears/Earlobes			Calves		
Neck			Knees		
Shoulders			Ankles		
Breasts – Shape			Feet in general		
Breasts – Size			Toes		
Belly					

Circle your favorite body part. Go ahead. Own it!

OK! Now we know what we're working with. Acceptance of the status quo right now is the Step 1. No two answers above will be the same, from any two women, by the way.

Let's individualize this, especially for you. Pick the top 3 from the exercises above, and list it below. We'll work with these in the next chapter, Step 2.

1. Messages from the past that impact me the most?		2. True or False answer that I need to pay attention to:	3. Body parts that I like or dislike the most.	
Message	Dark or Bright		Body Part	Like or Dislike
a.		a.	a.	
b.		b.	b.	
c.		c.	c.	

You're not alone if you feel betrayed by your body.

Even the most gorgeous of us suffers from body betrayal.

If you feel that your reflection in that airport mirror just can't possibly be you, you are not alone. At some level, we all torture ourselves about looking older.

When I was flirting with an attractive, sophisticated gentleman in the airport last week, he finally turned to me and chortled, while laughing at what I thought was my outrageously witty humor, "You even laugh like my Mother, and you look like her, too. You must be about the same age."

Need I say more?

Step One means acceptance right now:

- to accept messages from our past about our bodies
- to accept life events that have shaped us - the good, the bad, the ugly
- to accept our attitude about ourselves and our bodies right now
- to accept the body parts that we like and we dislike.

Now, it's time to move beyond acceptance and adjust our attitudes so comments like the one above don't burn, and we can sally forth totally confidently in the fitting room, bedroom, boulevard, and the board room.

Bring your short list above, and let's dive into Step 2, Adjust.

"Everything in life that we really accept undergoes a change"
– KATHERINE MANSFIELD

Step 2.
Adjust

*"YOUGOTTA
WANNA
WANNA"*

- KAT FORSYTHE

In Step 2, our job is to command that the voices of doubt take a hike while we adjust our attitudes (otherwise known as mood, disposition, vibes, energy, 'tude) so we can luxuriate in our own zestiness..

Yep. Easier said than done, but that doesn't mean it can't be done. However, you've got to want to do it. More precisely said,

"Yougottawannawanna".

It comes down to this:
- How you present yourself
- The confidence that you articulate
- The zestiness you exhibit

is simply all about the attitude that you bring to the party. Sometimes our attitude transformations are minor adjustments.

Sometimes it's a major overhaul. Doesn't matter. Without attitude transformation, nothing else matters. You simply must be at the right attitude to be your beautiful, real, fun, zesty, sexy, authentic self.

In this step, we'll examine all the ways we can adjust our attitudes and free up more personal space to savor who we are right now.

Monitor Your Thinking

Very important: The good news is that your attitude can be transformed and adjusted rather easily. Here's why:

Your brain believes everything you tell it.

Say something kind and complimentary about yourself and your brain believes you – and sets your statement into action.

"I refuse to think of them as chin hairs. I think of them as stray eyebrows."

—Janette Barber

The brain is very male in its singular interpretation of what you tell it. The brain doesn't ask how you *really* feel about it, or if you'd like to ask all your friends first. Nope, your brain is only concerned with the facts *that you supply for it.*

"I feel beautiful" is interpreted by your brain like this: "Ah, she feels beautiful. We will act beautiful. Set all systems to beautiful!"

On the other hand, if you say "I feel old and frumpy", the brain will react non-judgmentally with "We will act old and frumpy. Go get the old and frumpy mode!" You truly are what you think. The good news and the bad news about this are exactly the same:

You get to decide what you tell your brain. It's your choice. It will believe whatever you say.

I remember seeing a group of 10 German women in Eleuthera in the Bahamas, at Club Med, many years ago. They were topless, extremely overweight, and they were all in their 60's. Having the time of their lives, they were. Running, swimming, strutting and

"The secret of staying young is to live honestly, eat slowly and lie about your age"

– LUCILLE BALL

promenading on the beach without any sense of embarrassment or awkwardness in their bodies. You wanted to join them.

Interestingly, next to them on the beach were American women, also topless, with sculpted bodies, tiny bikinis, and tiny bodies. Great for eye candy – until they got off their blankets. The anxious unapproachable attitude in their gait screamed of insecurities and uneasiness. You wanted to stay away.

It's a lesson I'll never forget. It was all about how the German women carried themselves. It was their attitude that made you want to play with them. They looked sexy and provocative in spite of our youth centered measuring stick for body shape.

How do you get to be that comfortable in your own skin, your own body? How do you reclaim your body in the 2nd half of life? It's actually ridiculously simple. Let me show you.

Do me a favor. Stand up right where you are.

- Now, put your shoulders back,
- Tuck your butt under you,
- Lift your arms up to form a soft "Y" above your head,
- Thrust your chest out, lift your chin,
- Look up to the sky (or the ceiling),
- Take a deep breath.

Did you do it? When you do, you will notice an immediate mood change for the better, no matter how you're feeling right now. Why? Because your body likes feeling open, optimistic, and fully engaged.

Consider this:
- Just like you, your body likes to be liked and cared for.
- Like a magnificent garden, it needs to be cultivated to keep the weeds out and let the seeds of harvest grow.
- Constant vigilance is required.

- The weeds that hold us back are the fast growing damaging thoughts that crowd out the good thoughts.

Like weeds, those self-defeating, self-doubt, self-depreciating thoughts keep us from thinking optimistically, openly, and fully engaged.

What do you tell yourself in the fitting room? I know I'm prone to disclaimers (such as "I'm too fat for that. I can't wear that.") or saying something denigrating almost immediately with the first outfit that doesn't fit.

Last week, I was trying on shoes, black pumps in fact, and the top was cut deeply to reveal a kind of cleavage between my big toe and my first toe. My skin is not as supple as it used to be, which accounts for the massive wrinkled gathering of skin around the toe cleavage. It didn't look good.

I was mortified. I took them off at rocket speed before anyone else could comment "Ewwwww. What happened to your skin around your toes?" It looked old. I got depressed. I thought, "I remember seeing the skin gather at my mother's ankles, and she was in her 90's. I guess my days of buying low cut black pumps are over."

Enough is enough with those disclaimers and nasty thoughts! Mine only managed to ruin an otherwise entertaining afternoon of retail therapy. I thought about my crinkled skin for the rest of the afternoon.

Let's purge those gremlin thoughts right now! Let's temper our attitudes! Let's embrace these beautiful bodies of ours, just as they are.

"No one can make you feel inferior without your consent."
– ELEANOR ROOSEVELT

Be honest here. What do you say to yourself in the fitting room? What are your disclaimers?

✓	What I say (or something close to this). Add your own goodies in the blanks.	What I will replace it with
	I hate my arms.	
	This isn't age appropriate.	
	I need to camouflage my neck	
	OMG. Look at that Cellulite!	
	My stomach – really? How embarrassing.	
	This body is pathetic.	
	Please don't let the sales associate come in right now	
	I can't buy this until I lose weight	
	That muffin top is disgusting	
	Other:	

Do you say anything kind to yourself in fitting rooms? If so, do tell!

✓	Complimentary Comments from Me to Me
	I look wonderful in this color
	This makes me look thin (shorter, taller, longer waisted, sophisticated, successful, sexy, or _____ (fill in)
	I love how I look in this.
	I look beautiful!
	Other:

And, while we're at it, let's add your final list from the last Step (Step 1)

1. Messages from the past that impact me the most?		2. True or False answer that I need to pay attention to:	3. Body parts that I like and dislike the most.	
Message	Dark or Bright		Body Part	Like or Dislike
a.		a.	a.	
b.		b.	b.	
c.		c.	c.	

Now, we're ready to purge dark thoughts, rip out weeds of doubt, and slash negative thinking.

"A positive attitude may not solve all your problems, but it will annoy enough people to make it worth the effort."

– HERM ALBRIGHT, QUOTED IN READER'S DIGEST, JUNE 1995

"Don't compromise yourself. You are all you've got."

– JANIS JOPLIN, AMERICAN SINGER

Rule #1. DDD!
Don't Do Drama!

Truth told, most of us are drama queens from time to time. We make a much bigger deal out of things than we need to. The way to stop it is to stop it! When we repeat life stories of how hard it's been, how tough it's been being small/tall/fat/skinny/depressed/ill, how difficult it's been that our parents hurt us, how tough it is that our partner doesn't understand us. All drama! We get in our own way by making a romance novel crisis out of our lives.

Don't Do Drama. Simply stop the stories to yourself and others. Just stop.

Next time you're tempted to Do Drama, and have those weedy thoughts of, doubt, insecurity, disgust, anger, depression, and whatever else "ails ya'" (as my mother used to say!), here are techniques and tips to use to STOP the drama, cease the negative thoughts, and adjust your 'tude. Right now!

Tip 1: Thought stopping
Tip 2: End Relationship Smothering
Tip 3: Stop All Unnecessary Pleasing
Tip 4: Transform Your 'Tude - The Short List

Tip 1
THOUGHT STOPPING

Your car goes where your eyes go.

- THE ART OF RACING
IN THE RAIN BY
GARTH STEIN

Here's how it works —you stop your thinking right out loud with a forcefully voiced, "STOP!", and replace it immediately with a kinder, gentler, positive thought.

Here's the process:
1. Notice a thought that brings you down.
2. Say it out loud.
3. Clap your hands once and shout, "STOP!"
4. Replace it with a positive, kinder statement to yourself.

Here's the detail:

1. **Notice a thought that brings you down, that you say frequently. Some world class negative statements that make us feel physically worthless are:**

"She looks better than I do."

"He will never go out with me because I'm too old. (variation: Men our age only want younger women.)"

"I can never look good because I'm too _____
(fill in blank) fat, skinny, wrinkled, stressed, old, poor, unhealthy, grumpy, lonely, sad, etc."

2. **Write it here:**

Dark statement about yourself: _____
_____

Please notice how lousy you feel just writing it! Yuk.

"To be interested in the changing seasons is a happier state of mind than to be hopelessly in love with spring"

-GEORGE SANTAYANA

3. Say that nasty negative thought OUT LOUD.

4. When you finish, shout "STOP". Then, clap your hands once, LOUD AND HARD. Go ahead. Do it. Now, do it again, and mean it!

5. Finally, replace the statement with a kinder, complimentary, positive statement. For example:

   a. If you said, "I don't look good in formal gowns because my arms are loose and floppy". Then, you said, "STOP!" You'd now follow it by saying something positive. Like: "I love wearing formal gowns, and I will find one that makes me feel wonderful".

6. **Now, write your positive statement as rebuttal to the negative.** Make sure it makes you feel good (even if you don't believe it right now. Remember how the brain is like a man – it believes everything literally, exactly as it is said, and weaves no other meaning into it).

Positive, complimentary statement about yourself, replacing the nasty, above: _____ _____

Please notice how much better you feel (even if you don't believe it at this moment. You will. Just keep doing it.)

Use "Thought Stopping" early and often to replace any negative thinking.

Tip 2
Stopping "Relationship" Smothering: when other people's opinion of you keeps you from doing what you want to do

"Enough is Enough"
-SONG SUNG BY
BARBARA STREISAND
AND DONNA SUMMERS

As women, most of us have been taught to P-L-E-A-S-E as our first priority in relationships. That's a bum rap because we can't possibly spend enough hours during the day pleasing all the people who are significant to us, that need pleasing. It sucks us dry for the trying. Worse yet, we *let* them do it. Yes, we do.

Learning to put the brakes on with "enough is enough" is critical for us as we exhale our body blues. Some women do this well. The rest of us react to these women who don't try to please everyone in two ways: we either label them as selfish, or we are in awe, and we wish we could emulate them.

Sometimes we women can be our own worst enemies. We sabotage each other. Truth told: we're jealous. I know you've seen it. Time to stop that, too. We're all in this together. So, from the women who actually set boundaries and are not pleasers, let's take a lesson.

Stopping All Unnecessary Pleasing

> *"If you want the rainbow, you've got to put up with the rain".*
> – DOLLY PARTON, SINGER

What do Women-who-don't-worry-about-pleasing do? Without any effort:

- they prune out the poison vines of relationships hurtful to them.
- they cubbyhole the people who drain them, who they can't prune back (partners, children, parents, business associates)

These women:

- place a high value on themselves, their standards, and their time.
- they don't leak personal power
- they are miraculously free to spend time with people who count
- they explore and pursue the life they desire without *guilt*

These women place a high value on themselves and their personal commitments. They don't leak personal power. Consequently, they are miraculously free to spend time with the people who count, and explore the life they want in the style they desire.

Basically, you sense strength, grounding, and confidence from these women. Additional benefit: they attract significant relationships who value and respect their time, talents, and their needs. Know anyone like this? I sure do, and I adore hanging out with her. She raises me to her level.

For the rest of us, we could use a little guidance and encouragement to dump the drainers and cubbyhole the others. We need a boost to encourage and energize us stop pleasing the whole darn world!

GO FOR THE BEST AND FORGET THE REST! DO THE SIGNIFICANT RELATIONSHIP INVENTORY AND ACTION PLAN ASAP.

Fill out the Significant Relationship Inventory and Action Plan on this page and the next page. Identify where you want to stop, start, or continue with relationships in your life.

Allow yourself more freedom—and less pleasing.

Please note "when" on the Action Plan on the next page. Making a time commitment makes it real—and makes you accountable. Remember, your brain will follow directions. Even if you don't act on it immediately, you will have placed the suggestion of what you want to do in your consciousness. You'll be surprised by how fast your brain will act on it.

"If you tell the truth, you don't have to remember anything."
— MARK TWAIN

Part One: Significant Relationship Inventory – surrounding myself with the BEST

From this day forward (today's date: _____), I will make a commitment to let go of over pleasing. I commit to consciously identify and surround myself with people that support me, build my energy, and make me feel wonder-full without having to please them. These are people who encourage me, nourish me and I do the same for them. That means dumping or "cubbyholing" people who drain my energy.

Part 2: Significant Relationship Inventory and Action Plan

I will STOP these relationships (dump or cubbyhole)

Who?	Action I will take	When
1.		
2.		
3.		

I will START relationships with these new people

Who?	Action I will take	When
1.		
2.		
3.		

I will CONTINUE nurturing relationships with these people

Who?	Action I will take	When
1.		
2.		
3.		

The bottom line here:

Let go of the downers in your life, court the people who energize you—and watch your zest and joie de vivre soar!

 Voila! You're freed up to be the confident woman that you are. Just watch how much more assertive you will be when it comes to stepping out and articulating your delicious zestiness at midlife and beyond.

Imagine: No more buying that thing you don't really like just to please your boyfriend, or eating your 90 year old Great Aunt Bessie's mincemeat pie you've always hated, or listening to your grandchild begging to stay up late when you crave some peace and quiet.

Done with that! All it takes is a simple "No thank you. Not today."

Suddenly, you're not pleasing everyone.

Own it!

"Life is a shipwreck but we must not forget to sing in the lifeboats."

–VOLTAIRE

Transform your 'Tude and your Life will Follow.

The Short List of Other Things that will Adjust your Attitude

1. Change your expectations.
2. Get more exercise.
3. Smile at everyone you see.
4. Give compliments to other women our age — even if they look like they don't need it. C'mon. We all need it.
5. Don't judge anyone. You just never know what is going on.
6. Read/Watch/Listen to humor. It changes your chemistry.
7. Do affirmations and appreciation lists. Tell yourself what you are grateful for.
8. Only wear clothes you love — Even at home when hangin' out.
9. Get professional help if you are insecure or depressed. Got temporary blues? Get a coach. Long-term sadness? Get a psychotherapist.

---

10. Give men a break.

Listen up, ladies. Most of the stories we create around men and motives are simply wrong. Men are hardwired differently than we are. They are singularly focused, and we are multi-taskers. Don't Do Drama! If you are obsessing about a man (and we all have at some moment in our lives), read this: Men are doing the best they can with what they have. Don't overthink it. Don't overjudge it. For the most part, they are what you see, and you're not going to change it.

The answer is in you, not him. Get comfortable in your own skin, get beyond your need for over-pleasing and let go of your need for this guy to do it right (i.e. do it your way). You don't need him in your life to make you happy. You need YOU in your life to make you happy.

> "I can only please one person a day. Today is not your day. Tomorrow doesn't look good, either."
>
> –MAGNET ON MY REFRIGERATOR

Many of you already know this. It's worth revisiting. The "battle of the sexes" is real. Doesn't have to be a battle, of course, but we do come at life differently. If a man is making you nuts, take a moment and inventory your personal investment. Are you more worried about his needs or yours? Are you waiting for him to make you happy?

Here's the truth: romantic love is an illusion. It's fun for a while, but it can't last. Long term love allows both parties to live to their full potential, honoring each unique style and needs. Let him be him, and let you be you.

If you feel tension, work out a compromise on how you'll handle it. Take care of yourself first and you'll see miracles in your relationship.

> *"It is only through disruptions and confusion that we grow, jarred out of ourselves by the collision of someone else's private world with our own."*
>
> – JOYCE CAROL OATES, WRITER

Let's move on to Step 3 where we start doing the fun stuff – playing around to feel even more attractive, spicy, zesty, and sexier. Let's go!

Looking back at Step 2, which of these will help you adjust to a fresh, forward-thinking strong attitude?

- Monitor your thinking
- Change your fitting room messages
- Don't Do Drama
- Use thought stopping
- Stop all unnecessary pleasing
- Evaluate the impact of significant relationships
- Monitor your "men" stories

Step 3.

Appreciate

"The function of music is to release us from the tyranny of conscious thought."

-THOMAS MOORE

To my long time dear friend,

Thanks for putting up with my nonsense all these years, and for working so hard for me to support me!

You are the best.

How can I ever repay you?

Isn't that what you would say to a best friend who went down to the mat for you year after year?

We're talking about someone who held you upright while you circled the drain with problems that may or may not have been significant?

Someone who you knew would always be there, even when you treated her poorly — even when you picked a fight, insulted her, ignored her, cut her off from your love.

Yes, ma'am. If this were another person — a good friend, you might treat her poorly from time to time, but eventually, you would be filled with gratitude, indebtedness, love, and deep respect for all she had done for us. You would say, "Thanks".

Aren't you overdue to say that to your body?

Very few of us give this miraculous system the respect and treatment it has earned and deserves.

It's time to appreciate all that this overworked, underpaid, but always dedicated body has done for us. Remember staying up all night, when we were stressed about our children, our finances, rocky relationships, an illness, or our career? Who took the brunt of it — and bounced back, not always quickly, but bounced back, nonetheless? You got it! Our bodies.

A simple "thank you" will do. (Go ahead and say it).

Why does it matter, this saying thank you to your physical self?

It matters because now more than ever you need a strong partnership with your body. I don't know about you, but I'm facing changes in my body that I never expected, so soon, if ever. I assumed somehow that I would somehow dodge the sagging and drooping. Sound familiar?

When I see those bigger love handles and more belly cellulite, I convince myself that a good diet and more aerobics will nail it. Really? All those years of ongoing sit-ups, aren't doin' it for me. Will 200 sit-ups do it? No. Yes, it may tighten up the core, but it's not going to disappear completely, as it did in our 30's. Time for you and me to get real, redefine, and learn to look at our selves through a new lens.

"Some people don't dance, if they don't know who's singing,

Why ask your head, it's your hips that are swinging

Life's for us to enjoy

Woman, man, girl and boy,

Feel the pain, feel the joy!"

-From History Repeating by Dame Shirley Basse and the Propellerheads, 1997

Body Betrayal

"Everyday!"
-ANONYMOUS

Body betrayal means feeling let down by this machine that only 10 years ago ran a marathon, danced til dawn, had Olympic sex each weekend. Then, suddenly it quieted down. The old stamina just isn't there.

We're disappointed. We're frustrated.
We're angry. We're grieving.

We're blaming our bodies for what, in fact, nature is telling it to do. Yet, we demand more. We don't want to let go of the past, let alone face the frightening future of even more "age gain". It happens in varying degrees for all of us.

We have a choice.

We can protest "age gain"– and go down in desperate disappointment. Even with the best plastic surgery, the most intense exercise regimen, the sassiest clothes, the most expensive jewelry, the therapeutic facial and massage, the hottest make-up… changes are going to happen. In this youth centric culture of ours, that's hard.

Changes are going to happen. It's the darnedest thing, isn't it?

Exhaling means making peace with the frustrations and changes of age gain, and allowing new beauty, confidence, and joie d'vivre to bubble up from inside.

- Want resiliency?
- Want more energy?
- Want to look sexy, vital, and sensational?
- Want to feel really good about yourself in fitting rooms, on the street, in the presence of those evil tight skinned un-cellulited 25 year olds?

Start appreciating your body instead of criticizing it.

Any of a group of peptides occurring in the brain and vertebrate, and resembling opiates, that react with the brain's opiate receptors to raise the pain threshold and provide feelings of joy.
— EN-DOR-PHIN: NOUN.

Literally and figuratively say thank you to your body every day.

Like a dear friend, appreciate your body by furnishing it with what it needs to flourish and blossom for you in new ways. Start with saying thank you.

Did you see the movie "Water For Elephants"? If not, there is an elephant in the movie that is angry, mean, vengeful, and very dangerous. This animal is clearly bent on killing humans, and stays viciously chained.

One day, one of the trainers accidently says a word in Polish, and this elephant turns toward him. Turns out, this animal only knows commands in Polish! From that point on, as trainers speak in a language the animal understands, the elephant becomes docile, intelligent, obedient and helpful.

> *"Holding a grudge is like taking poison and hoping the other person dies."*
>
> –ANONYMOUS

He's responding to appreciation for his hard work because they're speaking a language he understands. Trainers begin to adorn the elephant with beautiful costumes. The elephant thrives — he struts and poses for the trainers. The team is a newly energized, well-oiled machine of understanding, co-operation, and appreciation.

So it goes with our body. We can hate it, punish it, abuse it, mock it, hide it, laugh at it. Or, we can understand it, reward it, care for it, groom it, adorn it, and adore it — and strut our stuff.

From your life wisdom, do tell:

Which is more effective at getting the long lasting results you want – Punishment or Praise?

Praise. Of course.

Let's start right now singing, praising and appreciating this body we live in. It's the only body we've got!

WHAT TO DO TO APPRECIATE YOUR BODY:
Body Appreciation Factors

If you are the human body belonging to a 50+ woman, what do you need to be appreciated?

"Change your expectations!"

-KAT FORSYTHE'S
MOTHER. APRIL 21, 1960

The Short List of Body Appreciation Factors:

1. Rest – 8 hours of sleep. Get meds if you can't sleep. Take a nap when you can.
2. Eat Good Food. You know this drill. Choose the right food. You know what it is. If you're ever unsure, ask your body what would help it most? Then listen. It will tell you. Try it.
3. Exercise – you know what to do with this one, too. Get your heart rate up. Lift some weights. Stretch out.

Your body wants you to work it.

You already know all 3 of these. Why don't you do them? It may be because you've never thought of them as:

- a critical factor for longevity in the second half of life.
- the key to youthful appearance and attitude.

Your body needs to know you care!

The Short List of Body Appreciation Factors:

The Short List: The Big Three	Good for me! I do this now	Nope, not doing this.	Start it now (give me a date)
Rest			
Eat good food			
Exercise			

OK, that was easy, a good first start.

HOWEVER, like everything else in life, there are no free lunches. Are you sincere and earnest in wanting to exhale your body blues, coming to peace with the changes, and wanting to look and feel fabulous?

There's more work to be done. Move on to the "Now I'm Serious" list below.

Pick the Body Appreciation Factor that speaks to you. Make your body hum! An appreciated body is a happy body with a self-assured, sensational owner (that would be you). You'll see.

Own it!

"NOW I'M SERIOUS!" BODY APPRECIATION FACTORS

For Me To Do	FACTORS	More Discussion on Page Listing Below.
	1. Keep your attitude positive. Get the right lens and start seeing anew.	48
	2. Pay Attention to all 5 of your senses. Now that's sensuous!	50
	3. Drape and adorn with ease and assurance	55
	4. Manage Modern Stress.	55
	5. Be who you are. Your body wants you to be real!	57
	6. Make new friends but keep the old.	59
	7. Say what you know.	59
	8. Be sexy. This is not complicated.	59
	9. Laugh. You know this already.	59
	10. Cry. Let it out. Don't hold back.	60
	11. Smile at people. Everyone feels better, starting with you.	60
	12. Spend time by yourself out of the house.	60
	13. Stand up straight. Sit up straight. Slouching is not sexy.	60
	14. Get professional help if you can't shake the blues for more than a month.	61
	15. Be silly. Actually being silly is serious stuff.	61

"Change your Face!"
(meaning watch your
facial expression)

- Kat Forsythe's
mother, April 22, 1960

1. Keep your attitude positive.

Get the right lens and start seeing anew.

Your body operates best when you are happy. That's just the way it is. When your body is happy, you walk with assurance, pride, and beauty. Start seeing things through a lens of optimism. Do it today.

- Quit complaining and start saying thank you.
- Quiet the brain chatter.
- Change your expectations
- Affirmations and gratitudes that you can't afford to miss
- Judge not. We all hide what's really going on.

Quit complaining and start saying thank you.

This is really simple.

- Listen to the words you use. Remember, your brain believes whatever you tell it. Most of us complain much too much. My mother used to say, "We like people for what they are, not for what they aren't". Complaining only brings you down. Unless complaining will lead to change directly, don't do it.
- Start saying thank you – to your body and everything else. When you are walking down the street at rocket speed, and you are getting tired, but you have to get to that meeting because you're already running late, say "thanks, body, for helping me out, here. I promise a nap when we are finished".
- Be a team. On a team you have to say thank you to your teammates, or they get annoyed that you are taking all the time and never thanking them.

Quiet the brain chatter.

Monkey Brain. That's what it's called. The constant chatter of your brain. "I forgot the grocery list … I forgot to call Mom … Tom's peeved but I'm not texting him back …I've got to get those airline tickets … I'm so angry with myself that I ate that croissant. You know they're loaded with butter … well, you're fat anyway, so who cares? ... oh darn, here comes Fran. I don't want to talk to her. All she ever does is complain."

You know this exercise in futility? I know you do.

- When you start to go off in 50 different directions, STOP.
- Take a deep breath. Then exhale long and evenly.
- Close your eyes. Say, "What matters right now?"
- Be gentle with yourself.
- Name one thing you are grateful for RIGHT NOW, even if it's just that Fran didn't see you, and you don't have to talk to her.

Change your expectations.

Perception is in the eyes of the beholder. If someone is really bugging you, or a situation is too much for you, ask yourself, "How can I change my expectations?" Then, change them. You can't change the person, or the situation, but you can change how you look at it.

Affirmations and gratitudes that you can't afford to miss.

We've heard so much about affirmations, going all the way back to Saturday Night Live with Phil Hartman in the mirror, and "By gosh, people like me." We laugh at affirmations, but the truth is that the brain believes what we tell it, remember? Say things to yourself like:

- ... I've been through things like this before, and I came through just fine. I can do this!
- ... I look beautiful in orange (or pink or purple or whatever color it is)
- ... Tom can be irritating, but I know he's doing the best he can, too.
- ... I'm so grateful for my feet, that they take the pounding I give them. Thanks, feet!

> *"Damn the torpedos, full speed ahead!"*
> -AUGUST 5, 1864.
> ADMIRAL DAVID
> GLASGOW FARRAGUT

Etc. you get it. Make your own list.

Judge not. We all hide what's really going on.

- This can be so darn difficult. When we are hurt, sad, rejected, angry – we want to strike out. Surely, it's someone else's fault.
- I have a friend who says, "We all walk with a limp." Isn't that the truth? When someone does/says/acts in a way that irritates us, just remember that most people aren't malicious, but they might be clumsy. Just being human with flaws like the rest of us. Anyway, when we take on judgment of others, it brings us down and it doesn't do a thing to them.
- We all hide behind a big cover up. You have yours. I have mine. Don't judge others for theirs. They're doing the best they can. Maybe not the way you would do it, but the best for them.
- Your body wants you to calm down so it can function well. When you take on judgement of others, you suck up energy that your body could have used to support you.

2. Pay Attention to all 5 of your senses.

Allow your body to operate at full speed.

- Literally, smell the roses!
- How about listening to some tunes?
- See the beauty around you. Get away from your computer.
- Touch everything and allow yourself to be touched.
- Savor when you taste.

Your 5 senses are your body's way of experiencing the world in full color. Reward it with using all 5 senses, every day. Find something pleasing in each arena. When you don't, you suffer from sensory deprivation that can lead to deep depression. Feeling down? Look to see which sense you are denying.

Literally, smell the roses! Your nose knows!

There is new evidence to believe that people break up partnerships because they are repulsed by the smell of the partner. Surprised?

Our sense of smell dictates our likes and dislikes, more than we know. Memories, creative ideas, moods, love making — all altered by smells. Our bodies smell aromas and interpret: caution or proceed. Most of the time, we ignore the messages.

As we exhale body blues and inhale new energy, the sense of smell is critical. It's critical to seek out the smells that make you feel nurtured, natural, comfortable, and confident. Be aware of them. What are they? Not the same for any 2 women. Roses? Bread baking? A certain perfume? Musk candles? Lavender? Search for the scents that you need right now. Watch your body respond and relax!

How about listening to some lively tunes? Are you intentionally listening to the sounds you love?

"If music be the food of love, play on" said Shakespeare in *Twelfth Night*. Music has the power to propel you out of one mood zone to another. You know that! Try this just before you need a joyful countenance - the fitting room, a big date, a visit with your children, or when you need a 'tude transformation. Get out your music source and play whatever catapults you to high spirits. Blast it. sing with it. Watch your body smile!

Your sense of Sight. See it for what it is! See the beauty around you.

- Too much time on the computer! Our brains crave the vision of peace and quiet away from the digital magnetic world of high tech. *Back away from the computer, and no one gets hurt.*
- Where does your brain get visual diversity?

"Almost always it is the fear of being ourselves that brings us to the mirror."
-ANTONIO PORCHIA

> *"My business is not to remake myself, but make the absolute best of what God has made."*
>
> – ROBERT BROWNING

- What colors turn you on? Surround yourself with them and wear them.
- Do you crave looking at nature? Go out for a walk.
- Get some flowers and pause to see the magnificence as you place them in your vase.
- Buy some fabulous art.
- We are such a visual world – and not always what you want to see. Don't watch violence – your body recoils.

Be aware of how you react to what you see.

Touch and Get touched. It's a matter of survival and longevity.

It's true. Lack of touch can cause deep depression, sensory deprivation of a great magnitude. We crave touching and being touched. Need a hug? There's a reason it feels so good. Living by yourself and no one touches you? Get a massage. Get touched.

Touching things we like can be bliss. Your favorite fabric next to your skin softly caressing you. Sheets you love to sleep in. The feel of your pet's fur when you stroke it. Find what you love and touch it! Your body will be ecstatic!

Taste it? Savor when you taste.

We can take a lesson from the French and the Italians. They don't taste when they dine. *They savor.* Savor the flavors in your mouth. Wine connoisseurs who fully understand the art of tasting tell us that the tongue senses in the front, the middle, and the back. Slow down and savor. Watch your body relax and relish the experience.

Celebrating our Senses

How do your senses help you define and articulate yourself as a beautiful, confident woman?

	Sensual Experiences	LOVE IT!	It's ok, not great	Does nothing for me
SIGHT	Seeing myself in my favorite outfit			
	Seeing other vital healthy women			
	My nails just after a manicure			
	Pictures of home			
	Pictures of my family			
	Watching a movie I love – adventure, romance, etc			
	Seeing myself in sexy lingerie or sleepwear			
	Watching children play			
	Seeing my partner's bare skin			
	Seeing/showing my own bare skin			
	Other -			
TOUCH	Certain fabrics against my skin – silk, cotton, wool			
	Texture of Nature (grass, flowers, dirt, etc)			
	Massage			
	Touching another's bare skin			
	Stroking my pet's fur			
	Other:			
	Other:			

(continued on next page)

Sensual Experiences	LOVE IT!	It's ok, not great	Does nothing for me
SOUND (HEARING)			
Certain music :			
Sounds of nature: ocean, wind, birds			
Voices of loved ones – siblings, children, friends			
Listening to poetry			
Partner's voice			
Sounds of deep breathing			
Other -			
SMELL (SCENTS)			
Newborn baby scents			
Baking or cooking, specifically:			
Your favorite perfume			
Your partner's body			
My pet's scent			
Other -			
TASTE			
Hot chocolate			
Family tradition foods:			
Coffee			
Turkey			
Sardines			
Other:			

3. Drape and adorn with ease and assurance.

Rule #1: Wear one item you love at all times. Even when you sleep. Wear what you love.

- See Step 4, "ADORN".

4. Manage Modern Stress.

Our parents had big stressors, but not like we do.
It's a full time job to keep stress at bay.
Cope with it, and your body will sing.
It's called Self Soothing.

Yes you can manage stress. No matter how overwhelming it is. Find a way to help yourself. No one else is going to do it for you. Here are my best suggestions.

1. **Lighten up.** Read/watch/listen to something funny. I have a copy of *Anguished English* by Richard Lederer next to my bed. It's a hilarious collection of mistakes, exaggerations, and accidental puns—and I can count on it to cheer me up. Get something like that.
2. **Let it go.** Take a deep breath and exhale. Do it right now as you read this. Now: Get over it. Not always easy, but sometimes you have to give it the "oh well!" treatment, and get it out of your life – or at least out of your mind. It's poisoning you. Would you continue to gobble down decaying food? Of course not. Don't continue to chew of decaying thoughts.
3. **Listen to motivational tapes.** That's why they're called that!
4. **Play your favorite music.** See "how about listening to some tunes" above.

"Living is a form of not being sure, not knowing how. … the artist never knows. We guess. We may be wrong, but we take leap after leap in the dark."

–AGNES DE MILLE

"The past is a great place and I don't want to erase it or to regret it, but I don't want to be its prisoner either"

— MICK JAGGER

5. **Change up the energy.** Get physically out of where you are right now, and put yourself in new place. Move that stagnant energy out of you.

6. **Call a friend who will kick your derriere and tell you to move on!**

7. **Read a romance novel**, or a murder thriller. Get distracted.

8. **Turn off the evening news!** Nothing is more depressing. "If it bleeds, it leads" is what sells and keeps us coming back. It's our obsession for bad news. Know that it's toxic to your body. Click "off" and go outside.

9. **Adopt an attitude of gratitude.** Thank someone or something for a special opportunity. Write a thank you note.

10. **Ask yourself, "What would I tell a friend to do?"** — and then go do that!

11. **DDD! Don't Do Drama!** You can break the stress cycle. Quit creating dramatic stories based on your fears, not reality. You simply must want to stop the drama. It's addictive. Don't be a drama junkie.

5. Be who you are.
Your body wants you to express your individuality.
We all bring special unique qualities to life.
Don't pressure yourself to be something you aren't.
Honor your uniqueness.

Know yourself well? There are many ways to "show up" in life. Honor yours!

WHICH ARE YOU? EXTRAVERT OR INTROVERT? BOTH HAVE STRENGTHS...

✓	EXTRAVERT	✓	INTROVERT
	Uses many words quickly.		Economical with words.
	Wants to **talk** it out, think out loud using **train of consciousness.**		Wants to **think** it out – thinks to him/herself first, then **maybe** talk.
	Silence is embarrassing.		Silence is a blessing.
	Fragmented, easily distracted.		Concentrated focus.
	Pulled outward (often in spite of him/herself). Gets energy externally.		Pulled inward (often in spite of him/herself). Gets energy internally.
	Enthusiastic, animated demeanor.		Calm, measured, reserved demeanor.
	Interrupts and finishes sentences for others.		Starts conversation without a preface (gets right to the point).
	Fast, immediate responses.		Slow, thoughtful responses.
	Comments reveal the **beginning parts** of the extravert's thought process.		Comments are the **end parts** of introvert's thought process.
	Tunes in quickly to outside world (tend to ignore inner dialogue). Sensitive to who and what is around him/her.		Tunes into the inner dialogue (tends to be less sensitive to outside world influences).

(continued on next page)

✓	EXTRAVERT	✓	INTROVERT
	Drained or bored if alone too much.		Too much time with others, especially strangers, is draining.
	Figures out things by talking over with others. Likes brainstorming.		Figures out things by thinking to him/herself. Dislikes brainstorming.
	At meetings, speaks out early & often.		At meetings, may hold back – then has trouble getting into discussion.
	Likely to speak first and think later – "foot in mouth".		Likely to think afterwards of the thing to say – "why didn't I say…".
	May prefer presenting ideas verbally rather than in writing.		May prefer presenting ideas in writing rather than verbally.
	Is generally easy to get to know –shows the world who he/she really is. Likes self-disclosure early.		Has a hidden side – can surprise people. May be difficult to get to know. Dislikes self-disclosure.
	Public.		Private.
	In meetings, ideas may be "half-baked". Likes talking to build ideas.		In meetings, verbalized ideas have been thought through thoroughly.
	Enjoys introducing people and then stays to make the conversation "work".		Prefers to be introduced (not to do the introducing). If forced to introduce, may leave conversation after introduction.
	The first hand up in group discussion.		The last hand up (or never) in group discussion.
	_____ Total		_____ Total

What's your "score"? Look at the traits in the column you favor. Are you living a life that honors those characteristics? If you're an extrovert, don't try to be an introvert, and vice versa. Your body wants you to be who you are! Authenticity makes your body behave for you!

6. "Make new friends but keep the old. One is silver. The other is gold." – Girl Scout Saying

"If you don't get everything you want, think of the things you don't get that you don't want."

-OSCAR WILDE

Friends sustain us. Nurture one new friend and one old buddy each day..

7. Say what you know.

You must have learned something in all these years. People need what you know. Share it. Daily.

How?

- Keep a journal
- Write a blog or make entries on Facebook. Call it "This I have learned."
- Write your life's story for your children, grandchildren, or for the world. Just write it! There is wisdom to be shared.

8. Be sexy.

This is not complicated.

- Yup. Be sexy – whatever that means to you.
- Just decide you are sexy. Then, be sexy.
- Strut Your Stuff!

9. Laugh. You know this already.

- Laugh more. It changes your chemistry. Look at funny YouTubes. Read jokes.
- Your body loves this one.

"You miss 100% of the shots you do not take"

−Wayne Gretsky

10. Cry.

Let it out. Don't hold back.

- Your tears cleanse the poison inside of you.
- There's a reason for the saying, "Have a good cry, and feel better".

11. Smile at people.

Everyone feels better, starting with you.

- Give compliments to other women every day and flash a big smile when you do it.
- Smile at people who don't need it. You simply never know.
- Your body loves when you give happinesst away.

12. Spend time by yourself out of the house.

- Take yourself on a date. Savor your solo retreat. Treat yourself as you would a guest.
- Go to a movie, out to dinner, to a museum, or a walk in the forest.
- Buy yourself a hot fudge sundae at the end of your adventure with yourself and no counting calories!

13. Stand up straight. Sit up straight.

Slouching is not sexy.

- Your mother was right.
- Good posture says you like your body, and your body smiles.
- Standing up straight speaks of confidence, wisdom, success, and beauty.

14. Get professional help if you can't shake the blues for more than a month.

- Go to a professional counselor, an MSW (Masters Social Work), MD or PhD psychotherapist who has advanced degrees in treating depression.
- Everyone will thank you (maybe not to your face).
- You will thank you.
- Your body will say, "Ahhh, that's a relief!" Holding in anger, resentment, jealousy, fear, anxiety and depression is poison to your body.

15. Be silly. Being silly is actually serious stuff.

- Play childlike games such as hide and seek - with a child, your pet, or another adult.
- Make up a word about yourself that describes you to you. Example: "fantabulous" That's you!
- Giggle in church.
- Go to a playground and swing.

There you have it! Appreciating your body simply means saying "thank you"!

Let's move on to Step 4.
Let's talk about Adorning this
magnificent body of ours!

"'Tis a gift to
be simple.

'Tis a gift to be free.

'Tis a gift to
come down

Where we ought to be.

And when we
find ourselves

In the place
that's right,

'Twill be in the valley

Of love and delight."

-NINETEENTH CENTURY
SHAKER HYMN

Step 4.

Adorn

"... for mature beauty is very different from youthful beauty. It demands a different approach. ... Mature beauty is knowing and sophisticated. It admits to effort. It is also richer and more complex."

—SOPHIA LOREN.

Wear only what you love!

When my father died, my mother remarried a dapper dude. Always dressed magnificently, he had enchanted me with his handsome haberdashery. He always looked so pulled together. One day, I asked him his secret to appearing so debonair. His answer was a blinding flash of the obvious:

"Wear only what you love."
He added this: "it must make you feel beautiful, or it doesn't belong on you."

Makes perfect sense, doesn't it? And it's so simple.

Why don't we do it? There are as many reasons as there are selections to choose from. Insecurity, habit, intimidation by advertising, fear of trying something new, fear of looking too young, fear of looking too old, wrong color, my partner doesn't like it (are you sure?), too expensive, not enough time, and on it goes.

What's your reason for not wearing what you love every day?

We're talking about adorning this magnificent body that we've accepted (Step 1), we've adjusted (step 2), we've appreciated (step 3) – Now we're ready to adorn it! We're all set to drape and decorate ourselves in the right way *that suits each of us individually*. That's going to be different for everyone, of course.

> Step 4 is about entering that fitting room, that summer party, that board meeting, that bedroom – overflowing with pride and confidence, with shoulders back, breasts out, head held high – with a smile for everyone, oozing self-assurance. How do you do that?

If you've done your homework, so far, you've learned the following, and you transport all of this into the fitting room with you (or any place on earth, for that matter), along with that armload of jeans, blouses and jackets. This is what you know:

1. *You bring a rich, deep life history with you, and you're darn proud of it! You've survived and thrived, thank you very much! (Step 1, Accept)*
2. *You know which body part you love, and which you want to minimize. (Step 1, Accept)*
3. *Attitude Transformation is easy to do with Thought Stopping, so that you get rid of crippling negativity. (Step 2, Adjust)*
4. *You Don't Do Drama! (Step 2, Adjust)*
5. *You're in high gear because you're sensitive to each of your 5 senses, and you're conscious of how the environment looks, smells, tastes, feels, and sounds. (Step 3, Appreciate)*
6. *You are about to don accoutrements that make you feel energized, confident, poised, powerful, a dab of sophisticated, and a dash of sexy You will settle for nothing less!*

"I don't want to look younger, I just want to look rested".
– MARISA BERENSON, MODEL

"Believe in yourself right from the start – believe in the magic that's inside your heart"

—THE WIZ

That's our positioning as we march forward into Step 4. Let's do it!

When we finish with Step 4, you'll be locked and loaded with even more poise, aplomb, and confidence. You'll take some deep full breaths and get a second wind. You'll exhale and **rejubilate** (reclaim jubilation, elation and joy) about your brilliant body!

In Step 4, here's what you'll find out:

1. What's your look? Get onboard with you. Not talking about fashion trends, here. The focus is this: What are the words YOU would describe YOUR OWN PERSONAL EXPRESSION OF YOU.
   - Do the garments that touch your skin reflect the unique expression of you? Critically important! It's why some things "just don't feel right" even though they look good in the eyes of others.
   - Are you Tailored? Colorful? Conservative? Serious? Cute? Buttoned-down? Do the check list on the next page.

2. Know thyself when beautifying your body (dressing for any occasion). What's your natural body silhouette? No playing the great American comparison game, here! Know yourself, the design of your unique body, and the heck with anyone else. They're not wearing your clothes, anyway! You are!
(See page 67)

3. What to do about "I-hate-the-way-I-look-in-the mirror-in-the-fitting-room": A Plan for overcoming Fitting Room Fatigue.
(See page 68)

4. Tips from the experts for lookin' good, my friend!
(See page 69)

5. A few thoughts on closet cleaning. It's not a choice, it's a necessity. Closet casting-out is a non-negotiable.
(See page 70)

Let's start our body adornment with 2 easy, essential self-inventories.

Know Thyself! Check off the words that describe how you like to be perceived:

Athletic		Flashy		Orange	
Beautiful		Fluffy		Pink	
Black		Gentle		Plain	
Bright		Gray		Pretty	
Brown		Green		Proper	
Business Like		High Fashion		Purple	
Butch		Hippy		Red	
Buttoned Up		Leather		Sexy	
Casual		Loud		Soft	
Comfortable		Masculine		Sophisticated	
Conservative		Messy		Tomboy	
Cougar		Motherly		White	
Cute		Muted		Wild	
Feminine		Natural		Yellow	

Take this list into the fitting room and compare it to the clothes you are trying on. Buy what you love and suits you! Reclaim your look and own it!

Our next self-inventory involves our genetic code, adjusting our brains to get a grip on reality, and appreciating the authentic body design we were given.

WHAT'S YOUR NATURAL BODY SILHOUETTE?

No playing the great American comparison game, here! Know your own body design and the heck with anyone else.

I have yet to meet a woman who does not believe that her natural silhouette is lacking. Said another way: Everyone doesn't like something about her body! Guess what? There is no best silhouette. There is no best body shape.

Take the time to learn how you adorn your natural body shape. Discover how to articulate who you are as a woman – making the right choices that show off YOU!

1. Remember acceptance – your body was given the figure it has. Whatever your contour, cut your body some slack, and praise it. Go ahead. Right now, a simple thank you will do.
2. Use thought stopping when that phrase "I hate this body" bubbles up. Just stop it!
3. Everyone is different. What enhances you will not work for others and vice versa.
4. All clothes are designed by the manufacturer for a certain body type. It may not be your type. Mannequins have no life. You do! Don't compare yourself to something without a heart beat.

Not even the super models are the same!
Understanding your silhouette helps you understand
how to adorn yourself beautifully.
Knowledge is power!

For example, I have long legs that go with my long body. I also have knees that are "non-traditional". I wear long skirts, great jeans, and skirts with tights. You will not see me in shorts that reveal the knees. Why would I do that? I have other lovely features to accentuate!

Here we go. You are *basically* one of these geometric silhouettes.

Use the information on the next page to flatter, flourish, and be fabulous.

What's Your Body Silhouette?
Flatter, Flourish, and Fabulous! Own it!

Triangle:

You've got fabulous hips and narrower shoulders. Keep the bottom simple and jazz up the top with wide collars and large lapels. Separates work well. Stay away from frills or pleating.

Inverted Triangle:

You've got wider shoulders and narrower hips. Keep top simple and focus on the bottoms. Make sure top covers the bottom (literally!). Thin straps will show off your shoulders – but if you want to hide them, go for plain tops and fancy bottoms.

Rectangle:

Your athletic contour looks wonderful in feminine tops and blazers with lots of darts and curves. Create an illusion of curves with kick outs on tops. No vertical stripes for you but you can wear horizontal stripes beautifully. Tight clothing needs belts to show curves.

Oval:

Your warm silhouette wants to flatter your eyes. Your focus is on your face and your neckline. You show off wonderful jewelry easily. Monochromatic tops and bottoms will point up your lovely eyes. Flowy clothes move easily with your silhouette. Go for slight flare on bottoms. Wear heels or long boots to lengthen you.

Hourglass:

Think Marilyn Monroe. Shoulder and hips are generally equal. Your waist is your great asset! Show it off! Single pieces need a belt. Pencil skirts look best when they hit right at the knee. Scoop or V-neck will point right at your terrific waist. No full bottoms – they detract from that amazing waist.

Know Thyself!

Handling Fitting Room Fatigue

Even the most self-confident women I know have fitting room challenges. That outfit looked so good on the mannequin. Don't let disappointment in the fitting room bring you down, or create depression. Stand tall! Here's how to arm yourself for the fitting room.

A PLAN FOR OVERCOMING FITTING ROOM FATIGUE

Remember the Paul Simon song in which he says, "Make a plan, Stan!"? There is no better place for a plan than the fitting room. Girl Scouts say, "be prepared". This is it! The next time you're alone in a fitting room with a stack of clothes that looked fabulous on the mannequin, do this.

Get your head screwed on right *before* you enter the dressing room. Then, take a deep breath, exhale slowly.

1. Rule #1 for ever and ever: Try on and buy only what you love. Nothing else counts.
2. Don't ask anyone if an outfit makes you look fat. If you have to ask, it doesn't matter what the answer is. You'll never wear it.
3. Ask yourself, *"Do I feel wonderful in this?"* NOT: *"Do I look good?"* Big difference. Feeling wonderful is an uplifting surge that comes from within. Looking good is a judgement from the outside. Whether you're buying bras, earrings, or a suit for the office, your answer should always be "YES, I feel wonderful." Any other answer means DON'T BUY IT.
4. Thought stopping! Immediately stop the nasty self-deprecating thoughts when they start. Have zero tolerance for them! Clap your hands and say, "NO!".
5. Be real. You're not 25, and thank heaven you're not. Now, have fun, be a little daring, and show off that wise, savvy, vibrant woman that you have waited to become, all these amazing years.
6. Can we let go of the size thing? *Don't let size determine whether you buy it or not.* When you get home, cut out the tag. It's only a guide, anyway. Every manufacturer sizes differently.
7. Don't buy what the sales associate says looks good. BUY ONLY WHAT *YOU* LOVE and buy only what makes you feel lovely.
8 If you are in HALT (Hungry, Angry, Lonely, Tired), you won't make good decisions. Consider taking a nap instead. Go home and come back to the fitting room at another time.

Here's what the pros say about adorning our bodies. Tried
and true advice, my beautiful friends. Listen up!

TIPS FROM THE EXPERTS FOR LOOKIN' GOOD, MY FRIEND!

1. Buy and wear only what you love. (Heard that before somewhere?)
2. Know what looks good on you. Buy it again. And again. It'll never go out of style because it looks good on you.
3. Buy the best you can afford.
4. Buy quality, not quantity. It will last longer. You will feel better in it. If you shop in resale shops, enter telling yourself you are there to feel pampered and lovely. Never enter telling yourself that you will find a "deal". "Deals" are for cars. "Lovely" is for adorning yourself.
5. When shopping, watch out for trends. Don't be pressured by them. If they compliment you, go for it. Otherwise, turn a blind eye and a deaf ear to them. Be brave. Stand up against the tyranny of the shoulds! Stick with your style.
6. Love what you buy but don't let the emotion of the moment lead you to buy something you regret later.
7. Take care of your adornments (clothes). When they are clean and pressed, you feel stronger, more confident, and zesty. The Colombo look is not cool.
8. Keep your hair clean, beautiful, and styled. Get expert advice on what looks good on you. Don't get stuck in a hairstyle you wore 30 years ago - unless you *want* to look like you stepped out of a time warp.
9. Don't buy shoes you can't walk in. Truth told, we've all done it. Resist the urge. Nothing looks so amazing that you should sacrifice pain for comfort. No, they won't stretch out that much. Think about our discussion of appreciating your body—your body needs you to love it, not punish it. There will be other shoes. Lots of them, in fact! Keep looking.
10. Invest in undergarments that make you feel incredibly sensual and happy. You want luxury and loveliness next to your skin. Watch yourself smile. No one will know - but you will.
11. Always wear only what you love – clothes, coats, shoes, jewelry. (Is there an echo in here?)

"Say No to 1000 things. It's only when you say no that you can concentrate on the things that are really important."

—STEVE JOBS

Do Something About Your Closet!

No wiggle room here. Get the old stuff out of your closet. Do it today. Start now.

Create space for your new wardrobe, the new you. Those old things that hang around (literally) are sucking up your new revitalized energy. You already know that! Pitch that old stuff.

What's cluttering up your closet that needs to be gone? Here's what women typically tell me:

- Old "event" clothes with sentimental value (daughter's wedding, etc.)
- Expensive had-to-have items you've never once worn.
- Something that will fit one day
- Shoes – look incredibly cool – don't fit
- Purses – too big, small, worn, bad color
- Things that don't match
- Impulse items
- Guilt gift items you will never wear (birthday from boyfriend, final gift from mother, etc.)

What's in your closet that needs to go 6 feet under? Why don't you do something about it?

Here's the challenge: Resistance to your changing body keeps you from dumping the old, the obsolete, the tired, and the outdated attire in your wardrobe.

You and I and all of my clients suffer from the same fantasy: We keep hoping it will fit again. Even if it does fit again some day, it's guaranteed to look stale and antiquated, whether you want to admit it or not.

Step up to the plate and re-energize your closet, your attitude, and your body with new lovely clothes. Reward yourself. Get new things that represent the fresh, vibrant you that you are today.

We all wear 20% of what we have in our closet. Think about it. It takes precious energy trying to sift through the other 80%. How many times have you decided to wear an older outfit, thinking it still fits? Then, in the midst of your day, you catch a glimpse in the mirror. Not the vision of yourself that you'd like to see!

Exhale those body blues, and create space for your current forward-thinking life. Get the old stuff out. You deserve it! Don't settle for less.

"You have to like who you are."
–Eileen Ford

Three Words about Color

Don't wear black. Seriously, stop wearing so much black. There is a whole rainbow of color waiting for you. Did you know that black repels people? If you want to be warm and approachable, let new colors into your wardrobe. Blue is universal. Orange suits most everyone. If black has become your uniform, spice it up with colorful scarves. Get color next to your face. Color tells the world that you are vital, strong, and assertive.

Change it up! Color yourself confident, spirited, and joyful.

Adorning the Epidermis

Did you know that the skin is the largest organ in the body? It cries out to be cared for!

Skin takes the bumps and grinds of our clumsiness. It buffers our internal self from the poisons in our environment. It cools us down, and contracts to protect us from the cold. Like the rest of our body, it has earned the right to be adorned!

> *"We all have to go sometime, and when I go – I want to go with my high heels on."*
> –CARMEN DELL'OREFICE, SUPERMODEL.

The face has been subject to insults in the name of beauty since the search for the fountain of youth began, probably about the time of the Paleolithic cave paintings in France, 17,300 years ago! We have knowledge today that can change our skin from dull to radiant. Who knows what the long term affects really are? In the meantime, here are some make-up pointers to enhance our skin as we move past mid-life.

Make-up Secrets for Vibrant, Fresh Faces

1. **Start with a skin care make-over.** Go to a reputable store *and sit with a make-up artist who is close to your age.* Tell her/him that you are looking to highlight your best features and to look as *fresh and vibrant* as you can. Don't tell her/him that you want to look young. You might get scary 25 year old make-up. Pay attention and ask questions. Buy his/her products, or not. Do not attempt this at home parties unless you get private coaching from a pro. Group make-up classes have gone the route of plastic container parties. We outgrew them.

2. **Begin your makeup routine with primer.** Our skin dries and thins with age. Use skin primer. It fills in small wrinkles, making them less visible.

3. **Always use moisturizer under your foundation for skin plumping moisture.**

4. **Beautiful makeup requires a good magnifying mirror.**

5. **Where are your eyebrows?** Eyebrows frame your face. We lose volume and color with age. Match your eyebrow pencil to your hair color before graying.

6. **No more bleeding lip color.** Coat the lips with foundation before applying lipstick to keep color from bleeding or use all day color lipstick.

7. **Moist lips are sexy lips.** No more dry, flaky lips. Moisturize often using lip balms with shey butter, petroleum jelly, or vitamin E. Be sure your lip balm has sunscreen.

8. **Whiten those teeth.** You're local drugstore has plenty of whiteners. Have it done professionally by your dentist to get it done quickly.

9. **Perk up tired eyes.** Get more rest. Sleep triggers the release of hormones that help the skin remain thicker and more elastic. Salt and carbonated beverages are culprits that swell eyes. Stay away from them.

10. **Wear sunglasses.** Not only will you look hip, slick and cool, but sunglasses protect the delicate skin around the eyes from sun damage. You'll squint less and create less wrinkles around your eyes. Medically, sunglasses may help to delay cataracts as well.

11. **Exfoliate that dead skin!** Get yourself a loofah (rough sponge) and exfoliating cleanser. Gently scrub your face and body.

12. **Moisturize your hands.** Hands look plumper and more youthful with lots of lotion. Put extra moisturizer on cuticles. Carry lotion with you at all times.

13. **Don't smoke.** Tobacco smoke releases an enzyme that breaks down collagen and elastin, components that are vital to the skin's structure, elasticity, and youthfulness.

14. **Use sunscreen every day.**

Say thank you to your visage. It's the greeting that the world sees first.

We've adorned you! You look radiant, vibrant, and a bit playful. Take a deep breath, get a second wind, and EXHALE! Now, you're ready to OWN IT!

Our journey has taken through accepting our bodies today, adjusting our attitude, and appreciating these hard working bodies of ours. Now, we've adorned it.

- What words define your personal unique look? Are you "owning it" every time you step out in the world?
- What's your silhouette? What's the best way to decorate it?
- What's your plan to prevent fitting room fatigue? Do you feel be-you-tiful in the clothes you buy?

"Give me the luxuries of life and I will willingly do without the necessities."

–FRANK LLOYD WRIGHT

"When you get older, you build something else in your core, which goes beyond the physical, because it has to"

—MARISA BERENSON, MODEL

- What needs to disappear from your closet?
- Are you wearing only what you love?

Remember, it's not about needles or knives, salves or supplements, food or fitness. It's about what goes on between your ears. Your thoughts make all the difference.

After all, you're not getting older, you're getting started.

Now, let's admire the spectaculous, wonder-full you — new attitude, new adornments, new refreshed you!

Step 5 is Admiring Our New Selves.

Your Notes

Step 5.
Admire

"I base my fashion taste on what doesn't itch."

-GILDA RADNER

Admire: to regard with wonder, pleasure, or approval.

Our roadmap for Exhaling Body Blues has led us to Step 5, Admire. You're almost home.

At this point, it's about admiring this body you've accepted, adjusted, appreciated, and adorned. It's all about comfort and confidence in your own skin, and wearing that self-assurance with conviction. You've worked your way up to this point, don't stop now! Here we are —it's time to admire the results and the hard work!

Own It!

Take personal ownership of you and your body. Take the leap. Stand up tall. Shoulders back. Breasts up and out.

I hereby give you permission to proudly Own It! – your body, your attitude, yourself. To posture with pride and admire yourself in all of your day:

- the way you look in the morning
- the messages you give yourself
- the way you adorn yourself
- the way you walk away from the grocery checkout
- the way you talk to other women and men and children
- the way you step out and express your uniqueness in the world

"I was thought to be "stuck up". I wasn't. I was just sure of myself. This is and always has been an unforgivable quality to the unsure."

– BETTY DAVIS

Wait a minute, I hear doubts in the crowd. Let's freeze frame. Right now, some of you are thinking to yourself: In spite of all the motivation, logic, and practical methods you have given us, I'm still [pick one] FAT/ FLABBY / GOOSE NECKED / MUFFIN TOPPED/ DROOPYEYED / SNAKE SKINNED, etc. I'm still not going to feel good about wearing a bathing suit or learning that my 71 year old brother is dating a 40 year old.

Give me a break, how can I really feel wonderful about this body. Really?"

Here's the reality. Are there going to be younger women who have tighter bodies and quicker recall than you have? Yes. You will compete with them in jobs, for dating, for your significant other's attention, and hear comments from friends, children and lovers mentioning how good they look for their age.

"If one is a greyhound, why try to look like a Pekinese?"

– DAME EDITH SITWELL

You will ask yourself, "what am I, chopped liver?" Are there going to be pool party invitations that encourage you to bring your suit and join the "fun"? Yes. You will attend them and see the eeny weeny bikinis worn by 23 year old hotties. You will exclaim to yourself that there is no accounting for bad taste in these young women (except of course, if it's your own daughter). That will happen, *if you allow it to happen.*

Read my lips: It does not have to happen!

Here's the good news: You have a choice. You can succumb to jealousy of age. You can surrender to claims that needles, knives, salves, supplements, food, or fitness will win your youthfulness back by themselves. You can simply get despondent and throw a big tent over your miraculous body.

Or, you can call up your adult sensible self and understand that the only way to freedom from body blues and age gain happens first and only in your brain. It's all in what you believe. You can't halt time, but you can halt the time you spend thinking negative thoughts. You can increase the time you allow to love yourself all over.

Yes, you can admire yourself.

Discover your Your Courage Key

Does trusting in your own beauty come easily? No, not at first. For some of us, it's a full time job to keep our brains fed with loving, true messages.

It's really quite simple. All you need to do is capture Your Courage Key about yourself. Your Courage Key wraps it's arms around you, nurtures you, cuddles you, and then empowers you to stand up tall and tell show the whole world your splendor. Your unique Courage Key tells the demons of doubt to take a hike! Your Courage Key keeps you high above negativity and doubt, and encourages you to experience that glorious woman that you are.

> ## What's "Your Courage Key"?
>
> Your Courage Key is a simple 6 word statement that describes and empowers you every time you say it. It works when you, your body, and your brain are all in sync, when everyone on board courageously believes in YOU. When you say it to yourself, Your Courage Key sets off that special something in you that captures attention in a crowd, and makes you distinctive, in a way that's different than anyone else. This is written all over you: "I feel radiantly confident in my own skin." ... no matter what!
>
> Using Your Courage Key is the ultimate (and the only) formula for exhaling your mid-life (and beyond) body blues.

You are filled with your own wonder, confidence, talents. Once your brain has the courage to believe that, the sky is the limit. That's true for now and the rest of your life. Your Courage Key is what you've told your brain to believe about you and your body.

> *"How do you get to Carnegie Hall? Practice, practice, practice."*
>
> —ANONYMOUS

Own it!

But how?

How to Create your own personal Courage Key:

It's so easy — and it's essential! Look at the list on page 82-83. Check off 3 words that you believe about yourself when you are at your best. No one has to know what they are. You OWN these words!

When you say them to yourself, you feel strong, confident, and in charge — the world is your playground. They describe you, empower you when you say them, and fit you just right — like an outfit you wear that just makes you feel exceptional.

Your Courage Key allows you to admire yourself. Let's make this clear, however: admiring does not mean bragging. Our form of admiring takes place on the inside, and it shows on the outside subtly and understatedly. It works because it represents confident internal pleasure with yourself. Bragging, on the other hand, happens on the outside, precisely because there is very little pleasure, confidence, and internal dialog on the inside.

Are you serious?

Did you know it takes 20 days of repetition before a habit is broken or changed? Repeat your Courage Key for 20 consecutive days. Like everyone else in worthwhile in life, it takes time, commitment, shaking off doubt, and obstinate determination. After 20 days, watch your confidence, finesse, and savoir-faire soar.

The good news is that after you practice expressing Your Courage Key to yourself over and over, you do begin to feel the satisfaction, warmth, and trust of affirming who you really are. That's how it works.

Choose 3 words. No more. No less. If a word that makes you feel youthful and empowered is not here, please add it! Use a pencil – you will change your mind several times.

Congratulations on creating your own unique Courage Key. Say it over and over to yourself. Don't stop saying it.

Your Courage Key allows you to continually motivate yourself to be your best, and lets the world experience you at your best.

"In order to lead the orchestra, you have to turn your back on the crowd."

−ANONYMOUS

At my best, I am: (Check as many as apply. Then go back and choose 3.)

Accepting		Cool		A Good Listener	
Adorable		Creative		Graceful	
Approachable		Curious		Gracious	
Artistic		Dazzling		Happy	
Authentic		Delicious		Healthy	
Beautiful		Deserving		Hip	
Blissful		Devoted		Hopeful	
Bold		Dignified		Hot	
Brave		Diplomatic		In the Present	
Breezy		Effervescent		Inquisitive	
Bright		Elated		Insightful	
Bright-Eyed		Energizing		Inspiring	
Buoyant		Enjoyable		Intellectual	
Calm		Festive		Jaunty	
Carefree		Firey		Jazzy	
Charismatic		Friendly		Joyful	
Cheerful		Fulfilled		Jubilant	
Cheerleader		Fun		Juicy	
Colorful		Funny (make people laugh)		Kind	
Comfortable		Generous		Light Hearted	
Compassionate		Gentle		Lovely	
Confident		Giving		Loving	

Loyal		Quietly Confident		Succulent	
Luscious		Refreshing		Super	
Luxurious		Role Model		Sweet	
Magnificent		Sassy		Thankful	
Mighty		Sensational		Thriving	
Open		Sensual		Trend Setter	
Optimistic		Serene		Upbeat	
Organized		Sexy		Vibrant	
Passionate		Sizzling		Vital	
Peaceful		Smart		Warm	
Perfect		Sophisticated		Whole	
Permission Giver		Spicy		A Winner	
Playful		A Star		Worthy	
Proud		Strong		Zesty	
Quiet		Stylin'			

Here's Your Courage Key:

I am _____, _____, and _____.

> *"One doesn't discover new lands without consenting to lose sight of the shore for very long time."*
>
> –ANDRE GIDE

Admiring yourself shows up like this:

1. Giving and receiving compliments. Lots of them, every day, with a simple, two word, "Thank you." She who admires herself hands out compliments easily, graciously, and often. Not to please, but to share her rejubilation – the reclaiming of jubilation, elation, and joy - with others.

2. Use affirmations. Repeat your Courage Key as you put yourself out there in the world. First, place your Courage Key all over your house on sticky notes, or someplace you will see it regularly.
   - How about in your car?
   - On your office desk?
   - In your purse?
   - On your bathroom mirror?

Each day, start repeating it when putting on your make-up. Then, repeat as necessary throughout the day:
   - at work when you look in the mirror
   - at the airport, when you see your reflection (and watch yourself stand taller!)
   - at social gatherings, when confronted with a sassy 25 year old.
   - during intimacy with your lover.

Remember, the brain believes everything we tell it.

Admire yourself? Yes you can!

Now, let's march into our last stop, *Step 6: "Always" - How to Exhale Body Blues for the rest of your life.*

(Seriously, you really can!)

Your Notes

Step 6:
Always

"You only live once. 'If today were the last day of my life, would I want to do what I am about to do today?' And whenever the answer has been "NO" for too many days in a row, I know I need to change something."
—STEVE JOBS

How to Exhale Body Blues for the Rest of Your Life

The rest of your life? That's quite a promise!

The magic ingredient is Your Courage Key (and a few practical pointers). It's really that simple.

Your Courage Key — those 3 words that describe you from Step 5 - is the differentiating factor to propel you forward with confidence, vitality, and verve at midlife and beyond. It's the missing piece.

Why is Your Courage Key the solution for exhaling the blues for the rest of your life?

Your brain believes everything you tell it. Put strong, focused positive statements in your head, and you soar. Put weak, demeaning remarks in your head, and you sink. The words you tell your mind will make or break you. Your Courage Key is an affirmative, direct, focused, message to your brain about you at your very best.

I remember a grueling desert walking tour with my friend Susan Sullivan 9 months before she died of ovarian cancer. It was hot and dry, and we were all grumpy. The couple behind us commenced to fight – throwing verbal barbs viciously at each other. Everyone wanted to go back to the resort.

Susan stopped, let them pass, looked me in the eye, and said, **"We don't have time for negative energy. Why does it take cancer to see how blue the sky is? Let them pass.**

I don't let anyone or anything pull me down anymore. My days are numbered. I have time for only one thing - to love what counts: myself, my cancer, my body, my friends, my husband, my family, and my cat.

I'm a dynamic, vibrant, focused woman. That's my Courage Key – when I say that, I feel stronger. When I listen to that couple, I feel weaker. Let them go and let's focus on the blue, blue sky."

Susan's lesson has stayed with me all these years. A month before she passed, we were having coffee. She had her turban on her bald head. She reached her emaciated arm across the table, and took my hand. She gave me that familiar intent look one more time. Staring directly into my eyes, she pronounced, **"If I'm not afraid to die, you shouldn't be afraid to live. My courage key bought me 5 chances to live. I would have been gone long ago if I hadn't told myself every single day: 'I'm a dynamic, vibrant, focused woman.' Get yourself a courage key and go do life."**

Let's all remember what she said. All of our days are numbered. Get your courage key in place and "go do life". Every day.

"Sing in Full Voice"
- WHAT OPERA SINGERS DO WHEN THEY WANT TO SHOW JOY AND ELATION.

"Surround myself with the Best and Let the Rest Go!"

–SUSAN SULLIVAN'S ADVICE ON HOW TO LIVE THE FULLEST LIFE POSSIBLE WHEN SHE CONFRONTED CANCER.

Your brain is control central. It's a simple, neutral machine. You can control the messages that go in. Those messages will dictate the behavior, attitude, and emotions that come out. If you want to move forward positively, your brain needs that message.

A *few basic principles about monitoring what goes in to your brain:*

1. Your brain not only believes everything you tell it, it believes everything it sees. Your brain has no opinion except the one you give it. When your mother said, "It's just a movie.", she was wiser than she realized. Your brain needs to be told what's real and what's not.

2. Your brain registers a positive or negative reaction to what it sees – according to what you tell it. It remembers according to how you file experience. Liked that Billy Joel concert? Brain says, "I like this! Let's do it again." Disliked your holidays with your nasty brother in law? Brain says. "This is not good. Steer clear of this!".

3. "Garbage in, garbage out" – remember that from the early 1990s? We were talking about computers. The same is true of your brain. You become the message that you tell yourself. If you affirm the same message each day for the rest of your life, you will become that message. Your brain seeks consistency. If you put positive in, you'll get positive actions out.

How does that *sound* in real life?

You say, "My spouse and I will work out solutions in this new therapy". Your brain says, "Ready to refresh marriage. Open to new messages. Let's do it."

You say, "I will find a new boyfriend." Brain says, "Yes, Ma'am. On lookout for new boyfriend. Will sort out, focus, and expedite process. Give me specifics on what he looks like. I'll find him."

You say, " I look fresh and perky tonight." Brain says, " Set all systems to fresh and perky."

You say, "I will start Law School at age 62." Brain says, "I'm geared up for tight organization, and focused attention in law school ."

One of my favorite quotes:

**She who thinks she can,
and she who thinks she can't
– are both right.**

"You don't have time for negative thinking. Why does it take cancer to see how blue the sky is?"
– SUSAN SULLIVAN'S ADVICE ON HOW TO LIVE THE FULLEST LIFE POSSIBLE WHEN SHE CONFRONTED CANCER.

NOTE: The brain never says, "NO, YOU CAN'T". It does what you tell it.

Are you a corporate executive? Think of your brain as the Managing Director of your corpus (body). You're the Executive Director, and your brain manages your operations, and gets your instructions done. It implements your instructions.

All you need is that quick, simple phrase to refresh, restart, reboot, and kick start your brain to positive, for the rest of your life.

You need 3 simple words – Your Courage Key. Easy to use, easy to remember, and easy to repeat.

When you articulate Your Courage Key, you tell your head, your computer central, "This is who I am!". Your brain says, "Yes, Ma'am, Captain. All dials are reset to that!"

THUS ... it is imperative, non-negotiable, critical, vital, urgent, and otherwise essential that you get your head on straight, first, as you move forward in the second half of life. Define who you are. Believe it. Live it. Every single day, 24 – 7.

That means conscious, intentional, and vigilant awareness of what you're telling yourself. The new twist is: "Sticks and stones can break my bones, but the wrong words will *always* hurt me."

> "Don't you love it when someone incredibly beautiful like Linda Evans or Cindy Crawford tells us that the real beauty secret is finding your inner light? No shit. But I've done the same things these women have done to find my inner light and while it's true I'm happier, I still don't look like them."
>
> – MARIANNE WILLIAMSON

Will you forget to motivate yourself with Your Courage Key?

Of course you will. We all do. There will be times when nothing feels better than an old fashioned pity party. Give yourself that lonely party, if you need some wallowing time. We've all done it. Be armed with the knowledge, however, that your brain is absorbing this malfunction and it's resetting systems to "Sad". Circle the drain, if you have to, but get a life line out of there as quickly as you can. Linger, and you are bound to be even more miserable and attract misery around you.

There are other benefits of monitoring your thoughts, and keeping the garbage out:

- Your energy vibrates on a higher level when you are thinking solid, supportive thoughts.
- The right people show up in your life.
- Doors open to new opportunities where you never dreamed possible.

Don't waste anymore valuable time. Monitor what you think. Be the master, not the slave, to your thoughts. It's your choice. Start now! Use Your Courage Key every day.

Needles and Knives
Salves and Supplements
Food and Fitness

When your head trusts Your Courage Key – the 3 words that describe your best self – THEN, you can add all the facials, salves, rubs, buffs, exercise classes, foods, plastic surgeries you desire.

Salves and supplements, needles and knives, food and fitness – they're the arrows in your quiver to support your unwavering trust in the splendor of you, expressed through Your Courage Key. Each can help you retain your resolve to maintain your zestiness, in their own way.

There's nothing wrong with any creams, supplements, exercise, or surgery - as long as you understand that they're the auxiliary team, the back-up B team for your Courage Key. Each helper will be appropriate for a different time in your life. Some you will never use.

How do you choose the best auxiliary helper for you?

The golden rule for the use of any of these products or services is this:

Do unto yourself as you exclusively want to do unto yourself.

In other words, make the decision to use any treatments, products or services because you and you alone, have decided it's the right move for you. Don't let friends, doctors, magazine articles, boyfriends, children, spouses, dog, cats, mystics, or Madison Avenue persuade you. You have the internet, libraries, and an unquenchable thirst for the truth. Figure it out for yourself.

What if your doctor prescribes a medicine or supplement? Of course, if you have a life threatening condition, follow the prescribed path of a doctor whom you trust. However, always probe and ask questions.

It's your body, and you have every right to know how chemicals and supplements will interact with your body and the other meds you are taking.

"She who can laugh at herself will never cease to be amused."
–MAGNET ON MY REFRIGERATOR

> *"How far are you willing to go to get out of your own way, so that you can live the life you want to live?"*
>
> –JOSEPH HANSON, JR.

Ask until you get an answer. If they won't tell you, switch doctors. If you suspect something is wrong, ask. Doctors are people, too. They make mistakes. Be pro-active!

Keep in mind that no amount of medicines, vitamins, rubbing or buffing will sustain you, however, if your brain isn't in gear first. Turns out the power to set the stage for "anti-aging" is between your own ears – not in the fitting room, on a massage table, at the make-up counter, or in surgery.

Take a Big Bite of Life

Here's the key: You have to *want* to hear *from yourself* how wonderful you are, and overcome the barriers to believing it.

Step up to the plate in larger than life style. Take a big bite of life! Tell yourself some variations on these statements:

"I am worth rejubilating (restoring jubilation, elation, and joy about yourself)!"

"I care enough about my own happiness to let nothing get in my way of accepting, adjusting, appreciating, adorning, and admiring myself – for the rest of my life no matter what."

"Not anyone or anything will take away my personal power!"

We're nearing the end of our journey guide together.

I invite you to continue the journey by joining our vivacious community online.

Please connect with us at GetASecondWind.com.

Check out this quick reference list for you to help you as you move forward.

"Mingle a little folly with your wisdom; a little nonsense now and then is pleasant."

—HORACE, ROMAN POET AND SATIRIST

TOP TEN TIPS FOR EXHALING BODY BLUES

(and any other blues for that matter!)

1. **Say Your Courage Key until you feel it kicking in.**
   - For the first 20 days, say the Courage Key 3 times a day. It takes your brain 20 consecutive days to learn something new — and believe it.
   - After that, say it once a day everyday.
   - Change out the words when it starts to get old and tired.
   - Carry it with you on a 3x5 card, and on your smartphone. You can write it in code if you feel really odd carrying it around.
   - IMPORTANT: Say it before, during, and after any fitting room experience!

2. **Which step do you need to work on right now?**
   - ACCEPT where you are or where you've been?
   - ADJUST an attitude?
   - APPRECIATE your hard working body?

"Everything worthwhile takes time."

—AD FOR DIAMONDS FROM 1985

- ADORN yourself inside and out with beautiful thoughts and garments?
- ADMIRE your talents, your authentic self, and your accomplishments?
- ALWAYS — keep the right thoughts going for the rest of your life?

3. **Become very, very good at believing in yourself.**
   - Keep this journey guide next to your bed. Read whatever chapter you need to — whenever you need it.
   - Stick new motivational quotes in this book.
   - Make post-it notes from the quotes in this book. Stick them all over your house.

4. **Know — OFF THE TOP OF YOUR HEAD — what to say to yourself to blow off negativity.**
   - Right now, quick — What's your courage key? Tell me one mood altering, energy changing statement to say to yourself that you've learned from this handbook. Say, "yes, I can. Of course I can!" or use your courage key. Whatever you say, speak it loudly and with fervor.
   - Get up and MOVE if words don't change the energy. Do it immediately before you sink any lower.

5. **Keep your sense of humor, always.** When my mother was dying and she lay in coma, my daughter and I read funny stories to her, hoping she could hear them. Then, a miracle happened. Out of her coma, she opened her eyes, giggled for a millisecond, and said, "Oh my!" Then, she closed her eyes and we never heard from her again. Humor changes everything. Keep it handy.

6. **Wear only what you love!** Every day. Put on clothes that make you feel fabulous. Clean out your closet and free up your energy to be the new, revitalized, refreshed you.

7. **Know your authentic self.** Know your strengths and weaknesses. Ignorance is not bliss, ignorance is misfortune. Take a personality instrument and understand your own

idiosyncrasies. Self knowledge is power. It helps you know where your drama buttons are, when to back off, when to move forward, and when to throw in the towel.

8. **Share your life wisdom.** What have you learned that younger women don't know? Tell them (with sage gentleness). Write it down. Know that you bring a compendium of life understanding that needs to be shared. Who do you need to tell your story to?

9. **Be a part of an honest, sharing community of women.** Find a group of like minded women with whom you can relax and be yourself. It may take some time. If a group doesn't materialize, find a few friends to "coffee klatch" with. Relationships are what we do best. One word of warning: **Keep some things private.** In our attempt to please, we often say too much. Share freely, but keep a few things "close to the chest". My mother always said, "Breast your cards". That means that there are private things better not shared. You will know what those are.

10. **Never, never, never give up on yourself.** You are a beautiful woman from the inside out. Believe it. Live it. Hold your head high. Walk it out into the world!

"Once there was a little ol' ant. Thought he'd move a rubber tree plant. Everyone knows an ant can't move a rubber tree plant. But, he had high hopes. He had high apple, high up in the sky, hopes!

So, every time you're feelin' low, 'stead a lettin' go, just remember that ant.

Hey! There goes another rubber tree plant!"

-FRANK SINATRA
HIGH HOPES

"Those who think they can and those who think they can't are usually both right."

—Magnet on my refrigerator

It's your choice. Which will you choose? Loving yourself and your body. with all its new twists and wrinkles? Or will you resist?

At the end of the journey, we will, in fact, get older. Yep, the bodies we trusted for so long will run out of gas at some point, and will require more TLC than ever before. Nothing we can do about that!

What we can choose is our attitude and our beliefs about ourselves.

It's all up to you, after all.

Tell those voices of doubt to take a hike!

What's Your Courage Key? Say it again, and again. It's the formula that sets everything in motion and sets you free.

Dearest Reader,

We've taken a fruitful journey together in this guide, learning how to exhale body blues (and any other blues for that matter).

I'm honored to have shared it with you.

You've accepted.
  You've adjusted.
    You've appreciated.
    You've adorned.
      You've admired.
        You've got Your Courage Key for Always!

Congratulations!

Own It proudly.

Now, go "do" life!

You're not getting older, you're getting started!

Kat Forsythe

January 2013

"If you think you are beaten, you are.

If you think you dare not, you don't.

I you think you'd like to win, but think you can't, it's almost a cinch you won't.

For out in the world we find success begins with a woman's state of mind.

Life's battles don't always go to the stronger or faster woman.

But, sooner or later the one who wins - is the one who thinks she can."

—FROM GREETING CARD CIRCA 1980

Your Notes

GetASecondWind.com

Your Notes

Your Notes

GetASecondWind.com

www.ingramcontent.com/pod-product-compliance
Lightning Source LLC
Chambersburg PA
CBHW062032090426
42733CB00034B/2591